Secretly Un

When night time falls do you ever feel sad and lonely..?

Secretly Unhappy: please don't tell

Copyright © 2019 by Deonte Earl Towner

All rights reserved. This book or any portion thereof may not be reproduced or used in any manner whatsoever without the express written permission of the publisher except for the use of brief quotations in a book review.

Printed in the United States of America

First Printing, 2019

Instagram @deontetowner

www.deontetowner.com

Secretly Unhappy: please don't tell

I can't sleep.

Secretly Unhappy: please don't tell

Also by Deonte' Earl Towner

Poetry
Pieces in the Dark: Turn the Light On

For those that portray to be living their best life, but secretly cry all night behind closed doors tossing and turning with the covers and sheets all over the place, the alarm clock ringing reminding you to put back on your mask and pretend to be happy for all the people you are going to see throughout your day…

Dear late night thoughts,

I hate you with a burning passion.

You make me stay up all night overthinking everything. You give me anxiety when all I want to do is fall asleep. During the day my life is good but then at night you bring up every insecurity, pain, heartache, brokenness and then you throw it in my face. Why do you do that? You make me overcomplicate the joy that I have in my life. You take everything that is good and make it ugly. You take all my happiness and bring sadness. You enjoy seeing me toss and turn in my bed because you need someone else to stay up with you.

Why me?

I dread forcing myself to fall asleep at night because it is such a challenge. I wrestle against myself. I try to count sheep, but then it becomes too exhausting. I try to eat a late night snack, but then the thoughts still come back. I don't enjoy my late night television shows anymore because of you.

It is not fair.

I want my sleep back.

I want my mind back.

I don't want to stay up all night thinking about all the people that hurt me in the past. I want to move on… but my mind, body and spirit won't let me.

Sincerely,

the sleep deprived

2:00 AM

Late Night Thoughts

Secretly Unhappy: please don't tell

searching for reasons

When you left my life I kept replaying all the thoughts in my head. The good times we shared seemed to keep repeating in my mind. The thoughts of knowing that you are doing the same thing with someone else hurts me to the core. The way they look into your eyes, is the same way I looked into your eyes on that warm summer day. The way you make them feel secure is the same way you made me feel when I questioned your motives towards me. Will you vanish from their life the way you did mine? What if you truly mean what you say to them? Does that mean everything you told me was a lie? Maybe it wasn't a lie. Maybe you meant everything you told me. Maybe what you told me was only meant for just that season of my life. Maybe I am just looking for an excuse or reason to be mad at you because I am trying to keep your memory alive.

Maybe it wasn't your fault…

Maybe it wasn't my fault,

Maybe it was just life,

And now I am forced to move on while trying to cling on to every memory of you.

-Deonte' Earl Towner

Secretly Unhappy: please don't tell

Lying to myself

Sometimes throughout my day I tell myself that I do not need anything from you.

I do not need your kindness.

I do not need your love.

I do not need your warmth.

I do not need your sympathy.

I do not need your "It's going to be alright."

I do not need your hugs.

I do not need your kisses.

I do not need your touch on my body.

I do not need your late night text.

I do not need your early morning calls.

I do not need you cuddled next to me when we are watching a movie.

I do not need your pep talks when life gets hard..

But I do need you.. Do not cry! Breathe! You will get through this without them. We were a team, and I am tired of doing everything to prove to you that I am fine without you because I am not.

-Deonte' Earl Towner

Secretly Unhappy: please don't tell

Late night lurker

Even though I blocked you sometimes I go through your profile. I look at your pictures, your smile and I am trying to figure out if you are happier without me. I constantly compare myself to your potential lover in your pictures. I laugh and tell myself, "I look better."

I bet they don't make you laugh like I do.

I bet they don't make you feel warm on the inside.

And then I realize if all that was true then you would still be by my side.

If all that was true then we would still be together.

If all that was true then I wouldn't be in this situation. When will I accept the bitter truth? We are done and you are happier.

-Deonte' Earl Towner

Secretly Unhappy: please don't tell

the day will come

When we went our separate ways you told me you would always be there whenever I needed you.

I know that if I called you then you would answer.

I know that if I told you that I needed you to come over because I am having a mental break down then you would drop everything just to make sure that I wouldn't do anything to harm myself.

But I know one day you will have your own family.

One day you will have a new lover and you won't be able to be there for me like you did in the beginning.

One day you will send me straight to voicemail and respond a few days or maybe weeks later when I took care of the problem on my own. The pain cuts me deep because I know that day is coming, and I need to start preparing myself to be strong without you.

-Deonte' Earl Towner

Secretly Unhappy: please don't tell

perfect solitude

I need space from everything.

Life is going too fast for me right now. It feels like I am floating through life, and I am losing control. I do not have time to cry, think or reflect because too much is coming at once.

I need a soft place to lay.

I need to travel deep into a forest and go missing for a bit.

I need to turn off my phone and log off social media.

I need to lock my bedroom door, crawl into my covers and cancel life for a couple of days.

-Deonte' Earl Towner

Secretly Unhappy: please don't tell

I lose you win

When I wake up in the morning looking for your text I lose you.

When I go to sleep imagining your warm embrace I lose you.

When I am going through a life crisis and I reach for my phone I lose you.

Whenever I accomplish goals in my life and you aren't by my side I lose you.

When I turn on our favorite Netflix show and you aren't there to watch the next episode with me I lose you.

I never thought that letting go of you would be this difficult. When will I constantly stop losing you..?

-Deonte' Earl Towner

Secretly Unhappy: please don't tell

childhood says goodbye

I miss when I was younger.

I miss my parents driving me around everywhere.

I miss my grandma feeding me foods my parents told me that I couldn't eat.

I miss falling asleep in random places and waking up in a different setting than where I rested my head.

I miss my parents waking me up for school and telling me to have a blessed day.

I miss being able to see all my friends that I grew up with every day.

I miss being able to get passes for being irresponsible.

Now, everyone is getting older. People don't call like they used to. Everyone is moving on and living their best life away from me. People that I love are dying. Memories suck because they keep reminding me of the good times.

-Deonte' Earl Towner

Secretly Unhappy: please don't tell

nothing left to give

Can't force anyone to love you, no matter how many times you were there for them. The heart wants what the heart wants, and if their heart doesn't want you it is easy for them to look over all the things you've done for them. They will make you feel like you aren't good enough. You'll find yourself giving them the whole world and it's still not enough.

They will take everything from you, and you will have nothing left to give.

They will move on to the next person. You will find yourself on the floor broken into pieces because your love wasn't big enough to hold the relationship together.

-Deonte' Earl Towner

Secretly Unhappy: please don't tell

touching myself

Before you broke things off between us

you kissed me on the hand.

You told me to hold my hand against my cheek

whenever I felt lonely and you will be there.

As my new lover lays beside me I find myself touching my cheek, my chest, my thighs, my whole body every night missing everything about you until I fall asleep.

-Deonte' Earl Towner

Secretly Unhappy: please don't tell

fairytale endings

There was a time in my life I wanted the love I saw in movies.

I wanted the universe to stop once we shared our first kiss.

I wanted the animals to bow at our feet.

I wanted the butterflies in the sky to land on our ears while we held each other's hands and walked into the sunset.

I fell in love with you and everything changed.

You ruined all my hopes and dreams of ever being in love.

-Deonte' Earl Towner

Secretly Unhappy: please don't tell

love isn't fair

I fell in love with someone that keeps breaking my heart because they understand how fragile my heart is, and I allow them to get away with anything.

I want to love you until all the bad feelings go away. You moved on with your life, but I'm stuck with the memories that I do not want to move on from. I am stuck thinking about all the good times we shared together. I sometimes want to call you in the middle of the night and send you a random text about what we use to have.

I know that wouldn't change anything.

I know that wouldn't make me feel better. It will only make me sad because you wouldn't feel the love that I was trying to express over the phone.

-Deonte' Earl Towner

Secretly Unhappy: please don't tell

different type of hurt

The most painful experience is getting hurt by the person you risked it all for while everyone was judging them. You still stayed by their side because you wanted to prove to everyone that they were different, they showed you a side no one has seen but you.

-Deonte' Earl Towner

Secretly Unhappy: please don't tell

Forget Myself

Some people have been through so much to the point they forget who they are at night because they allow their mind to get them deep into their feelings. For some it is very hard to go to sleep and get out of bed because their past inner demons mentally drain them..

-Deonte' Earl Towner

Secretly Unhappy: please don't tell

texting in my feelings

If I could send you a text I wonder how it would go.

I wonder the response I would get from you.

I wonder if you would cave in and tell me that you miss me too.

I wonder if the feelings would be the same.

I wonder if my number is blocked.

I wonder if the new person you're in love with would respond and tell me to leave you alone.

I wonder if we would get back together and everything would be back to normal.

-Deonte' Earl Towner

Secretly Unhappy: please don't tell

only you

Sometimes I stare at the ceiling in the dark. I know that we aren't together anymore, but I keep having mixed feelings of how you ended things with me. You ended it all so fast but our relationship seemed so secure and strong. I never knew that you were hiding how you really felt about me. As my eyes keep shutting and opening because of tiredness I touch my chest in pain because my anxiety and depression is taking over my body. I breathe slowly trying to think happy thoughts but I can't because they are all with you..

-Deonte' Earl Towner

Secretly Unhappy: please don't tell

up alone

I just want to lay down for hours and not think of anything. Every night I search for peace, but it gets blown away by my cluttered mind. I tend to worry about things I shouldn't. I am constantly fighting my thoughts in my sleep. As the world is spinning all around me. I am losing control in my mind and slowly giving up.

-Deonte' Earl Towner

Secretly Unhappy: please don't tell

the blame game

I want to take full responsibility and accountability for the part I played in the relationship, but you are the one that did all the cheating and the game playing.

What do I have to take full responsibility for?

What do I have to say sorry for?

-Deonte' Earl Towner

Secretly Unhappy: please don't tell

benefit of the doubt

You made mistakes and hurt my feelings. I gave you many chances because I understood that people aren't perfect. I let go of everyone in my life so easily but I wanted to prove to myself that I could stand the test of time. I kept the hope alive because I was hoping that you would get yourself together. I watched you love your friends and family the way I desired to be loved by you.

Maybe this relationship was built on me being your punching bag.

Maybe you didn't look at me as the person you loved but instead someone that would carry all your emotional baggage.

Whenever you felt like dumping your stress on me I was there to allow it. I wanted some kind of attention from you even if it was bad but then I suffered in silence because I didn't want to draw you away even though your mind was on someone else.

-Deonte' Earl Towner

Secretly Unhappy: please don't tell

bring on the pain

I am used to getting hurt by other people. What if it is me that does the hurting this time? What if I have turned into all the people that have hurt me in the past? Maybe I do not know what I want anymore. Maybe I told you sweet things because it sounded good in the moment. Maybe for the rest of my life I need to be single because I have too much hurt and brokenness inside of me that will never go away.

-Deonte' Earl Towner

Secretly Unhappy: please don't tell

park bench

I'm thinking about you, but you're sitting right next to me thinking about someone else. You smile at me, but then you gaze looking the other way because you are too weak to end things with me. You do not want to hurt my feelings more than you've already hurt them. I feel the end is coming near.

Maybe you will stop calling me.

Maybe you will end things over text.

Maybe I will find out it's someone else through social media.

However, I find out I won't be ready and I won't recover.. but one thing that will never change is my love for you.

-Deonte' Earl Towner

Secretly Unhappy: please don't tell

ignore caller

I'll never forget the last week of summer when I kept sending you to voicemail. You sent me over ten voice messages crying because you wanted me back. We were both toxic for each other, and we were stopping each other from growing. I cared too much about you and myself to allow us to destroy each other. I wanted to answer the phone so badly and cry with you, but I knew that I would only accept you back into my life. This time I had to be strong. I couldn't allow you to keep coming back because it was making me into someone I wasn't.

I never screamed at someone until I met you.

I never walked away and avoided getting to the bottom of things until I met you.

I never allowed anyone to point in my face and call me names until I met you. In order for things to change then our paths have to change, and this path that we have to journey on doesn't involve us together anymore.

-Deonte' Earl Towner

Secretly Unhappy: please don't tell

secrets to the grave

There are stories I will never tell anyone. I will never forget how sad I was after it was over. I felt so scared and alone. I told one person and told them to never tell anyone. I became stronger and told certain family members and then I told some of my friends. After it happened it was hard to hold my head up and be strong. I felt empty on the inside, and I had to learn how to be me again. I was embarrassed, enraged and scared.

When it was all happening I couldn't use any of my accomplishments or status to stop what was happening. I felt powerless in a world that made me feel empowered. When people heard what happened some of them blamed me and said it never happened: only lying for attention. This world is so cruel and cold. I am no longer looking for warmth in other people anymore. From now on I will use myself for everything that I need.

-Deonte' Earl Towner

Secretly Unhappy: please don't tell

room for three

What do you do when you know that you aren't the only one but you don't want to walk away because your feelings are in too deep? What do you do when you have to start sharing the one you love with someone else? Should I show myself friendly to your other lover? Should I make you choose? I just want you to be happy, and if that means that I have to lower my standards then I will. This is something new for me and I was raised better than this. I am ashamed of how much I am willing to risk to stay with you.

-Deonte' Earl Towner

Secretly Unhappy: please don't tell

made up narratives

Sometimes I look at couples from afar off and wonder what their story is.

Is there relationship truly built on love?

Are they really happy?

Do they take pictures and look perfect on social media but they scream at each other behind closed doors?

Are one of them being unfaithful in the relationship?

Could it be true that they are soulmates and potentially perfect for each other?

Could it be that they were once happy but now they are fighting to make it work?

-Deonte' Earl Towner

Secretly Unhappy: please don't tell

delusional

I honestly don't want to know the truth.

If you are being unfaithful please do not let me find out.

If you are lying about how you feel about me please do not let me find out.

Allow me to think that everything is fine. Allow me to think that you really love me. I have been searching for love and with you it feels like I have it. Continue to act and be a part of my perfect love dream. Everything in my life has been taken away from me, so do not take away this moment of happiness that I so desperately want.

-Deonte' Earl Towner

Secretly Unhappy: please don't tell

war

When you're tired of loving my ex,

when you're tired of the games they play,

when you're tired of trying to be me,

when you're tired of the cheating. Fall down on your face, kiss my feet and beg me to show you how I did it.

-Deonte' Earl Towner

Secretly Unhappy: please don't tell

morning confusion

I looked in the mirror this morning and began to cry because I didn't know who I was anymore. I've become so wrapped inside of you I forgot about myself.

I forgot about what made me smile,

I forgot about what made me happy,

I forgot about the things I loved to do because I did everything to make you happy. You took everything away from me, and you allowed it. You never stopped me and said, "What can I do for you?"

-Deonte' Earl Towner

Secretly Unhappy: please don't tell

personal

"I hate myself.."

Says the one that makes everyone laugh, feel loved and encouraged.

-Deonte' Earl Towner

Secretly Unhappy: please don't tell

closed

Sometimes when you've been hurt so many times you forget how to open up again.

-Deonte' Earl Towner

Secretly Unhappy: please don't tell

cuddle season

I turned and asked, "What are we..?"

You looked at me in confusion and began to stutter.

Before you could say anything I changed the topic and kept watching our show. You began scrolling through your phone as though I never asked the question.

-Deonte' Earl Towner

Secretly Unhappy: please don't tell

sea of pain

Some people go to sleep in pain, wake up in pain, go to work in pain, go to school in pain, go to church in pain, in a relationship with pain.. and then the cycle repeats the next day.

-Deonte' Earl Towner

Secretly Unhappy: please don't tell

left me here

You are clearly doing everything in your power to distance yourself from me.

You keep apologizing.

You keep doing the opposite of everything you said you wouldn't do.

You keep canceling plans on me. In order for things to be over then I must hear it from your mouth that it is over. People keep telling me that a person doesn't have to officially say it's over for it to be over. At least give me the common courtesy and respect to lay it down easy.

-Deonte' Earl Towner

Secretly Unhappy: please don't tell

homeless

Sometimes people that have absolutely nothing are more grateful than people that have everything.

-Deonte' Earl Towner

Secretly Unhappy: please don't tell

workaholic

Some people stay busy so they don't have to deal with the pain they've been running from for years...

-Deonte' Earl Towner

Secretly Unhappy: please don't tell

no love allowed

I have struggled my whole life.

I do not know how to be happy anymore. Peace is foreign to me because I had to fight my whole life. All I had was myself and no one else. I have become so independent to the point I do not need love anymore. I am doing love a favor if I allow it in my heart. How can I move on from everything that I have been through? Pain was my experience and I am going to carry every ounce of it throughout my whole life.

-Deonte' Earl Towner

Secretly Unhappy: please don't tell

closure

We were sitting across from each other in my room. My eyes were filled with tears. All over my face you could read how emotionally exhausted I was. I missed you. I couldn't lie or deny it. You came over because you knew I needed closure.

You asked, "What do I have to do in order for you to move on?" I realized if I had one more dinner with you, one last kiss, one last touch of your fingers on my body.. it still wouldn't be enough. I needed to allow you to move on. If we could spend a whole day together doing everything that we used to enjoy doing it still wouldn't be enough. The feelings weren't the same anymore. I needed to accept the truth and allow you to move on. Hold on to the memories, but not live there anymore.

-Deonte' Earl Towner

Secretly Unhappy: please don't tell

sad hours

Even though I am in love, I still think about all my exes that did me wrong. I don't miss any of them, but I just get sad thinking about how low I felt during the time they all ended things with me.

-Deonte' Earl Towner

Secretly Unhappy: please don't tell

burden

How did you move on so fast?

How could you just treat me like I am a stranger off the street?

When I see you in public you don't speak to me unless I say something. I look at you, and I don't see nothing. I don't even see the love you have for me anymore. When you talk to me you look pass me like you are just trying to get this conversation over with. Every time I reach out to you it almost feels like I am a burden. My friends keep asking me why I keep texting you. I just want you to use me. I want some kind of attention from you. I don't care if it is good or bad. I just want you to acknowledge my presence.

-Deonte' Earl Towner

Secretly Unhappy: please don't tell

alone

Nobody sees how you treat me behind closed doors. They don't know how you abuse me. You pretend throughout our day that we are perfectly in love and then all of a sudden you begin the late night show. You shut the door, go on your end of the house and ignore me the whole night. I have become use to how you treat me, and this is what love is to me. You are everything I need in the day, but then at night I feel alone and cold.

No one there to hold me.

No one there to kiss me.

Just another body by my side that isn't capable of giving me what I emotionally need.

-Deonte' Earl Towner

Secretly Unhappy: please don't tell

same ol' mistakes

My mind has lost all its energy.

I begin to think that nothing matters anymore.

I begin to think about how hard life can be with all its surprises.

I begin to think why should I go through this day if all I am going to do is make the same mistakes.

I begin to think how everything seems to be the same every day.

-Deonte' Earl Towner

Secretly Unhappy: please don't tell

night cage

I feel too much at night.

My feelings are going to suffocate me and grip my heart until I am not longer on earth.

-Deonte' Earl Towner

Secretly Unhappy: please don't tell

use me up

You used me until you didn't need me anymore. I have no love left inside of me to offer another soul..

-Deonte' Earl Towner

Secretly Unhappy: please don't tell

sweet words

Stop telling me that I am going to be fine.

Stop telling me that I will find someone better.

Stop telling me that I can make it without you in tough times. You use to tell me that we were in this together. You use to be my strength when I was weak. I couldn't imagine going through a trial without you.

What if life gets too hard?

What if I call out your name and you aren't there to answer?

What does life mean without you? All that I know is you and me. Now all I have is me. I have become so dependent on you to the point I don't think I could live without you. I look into the mirror and my reflection reminds me that I am alone once again.

-Deonte' Earl Towner

Secretly Unhappy: please don't tell

side piece

When we were together you were in an open relationship and I was in a closed relationship. All along I thought I was the only one, but in reality I was sharing you with everyone.

-Deonte' Earl Towner

Secretly Unhappy: please don't tell

hold my bags

Don't let them tell you that you are taking too long to move on.

Don't let them stop you from grieving.

Don't let them make you feel weak minded if you need a few days, weeks, months or a year... take it because life goes on and you cannot move on if you are carrying all your baggage from the past. I tried to pretend that I was good because I wanted to put on a happy face for everyone else. My tears began to come out in different ways others couldn't see. I was no longer myself and every day I was turning into someone I didn't like because I never wanted others to judge me for my sadness. I kept quiet but on the inside I was filled with rage.

-Deonte' Earl Towner

Secretly Unhappy: please don't tell

can't swim

At night it feels like I am pushing against the waves of sadness.

I tell others that I feel whole on the inside,

but the waves begin aggressively raging in my soul and no matter how fast I try to swim away to the shore the waves take out its huge arms and pull me back in. I have given up. Now I am sinking, dying a slow and painful death.

-Deonte' Earl Towner

Secretly Unhappy: please don't tell

.

frown

People often say, "Anything that takes your peace away let it go."

How can it be that I am in love with someone that takes everything that is good away from me? I know better, but I do not want better if it involves you not in the picture anymore.

-Deonte' Earl Towner

Secretly Unhappy: please don't tell

give it up

Sometimes the person you're the most open with is the one that keeps hurting you. In the beginning you felt safe and now you're still holding on to the memories wishing they go back to how they use to be.

-Deonte' Earl Towner

Secretly Unhappy: please don't tell

sacred sacrifice

If you do not discover your worth they will end up leaving. You will feel empty and alone on the inside because you sacrificed your peace just to be with them. You will become bitter because lowering your standards and degrading yourself still won't make it work.

-Deonte' Earl Towner

Secretly Unhappy: please don't tell

Secretly Unhappy: please don't tell

Voicemail 0:01:43

Secretly Unhappy: please don't tell

promise

Congratulations,

I heard about your good news. I heard that life is becoming everything you've been praying for. Just know that I still think of you. There is not a day in the world that I do not think of you. I want the best for you. You deserve everything in the world. I am sorry that I wasn't able to give it to you. I am sorry that I didn't amount to everything I said I was. I let you down big time. You look so happy on your Instagram pictures.

I enjoy looking at your stories whenever I am on my lunch break. I remember how you use to put the camera right in my face whenever we would go out to eat. I remember when I would be driving down the road you would be on the passenger side secretly recording me.

You taught me how to live life. It sucks how I had to hurt you in order to grow as an individual. I will take everything you taught me in this last relationship and promise not to make those same mistakes with someone else.

-Deonte' Earl Towner

Secretly Unhappy: please don't tell

comfort

I heard about what happened to your pops. I am sorry about that. I know that we aren't as close like we used to be. If we were I would take you out to eat and hold you. I would kiss all over you and whisper in your ear about how you are going to be alright. I would remind you about how strong you are, but I know I would be crossing boundaries. I wouldn't want to trick your emotions. I don't want to manipulate you because I know that you are in a vulnerable place right now. I miss you. I just want you to be good, but I think this message is good enough. You can call me if you want, but I will do my best to keep it on a friendship level.

-Deonte' Earl Towner

Secretly Unhappy: please don't tell

i'm trying

Whenever you are ready to talk again I am here. I know you said that you needed your space, but I didn't think it would take this long.

Do you think we will get back together?

Or, are we done for good?

What if you want to be done, but I don't want to be done?

What if I want to continue what we had?

I am not willing to give up on us.

-Deonte' Earl Towner

Secretly Unhappy: please don't tell

overly available

I was a friend to you, but you could never show me the type of love that I would constantly give you.

Was I not good enough for you?

I answered every phone call on the first ring, answered every text message and showed up to your place to be there for you whenever you needed me. Maybe I made myself too overly available for you.

Maybe you wanted a challenge and I was too easy. So instead you searched for someone that is going to be strong and put their foot down.

Maybe you wanted someone to say "no" to you. Now I feel weak. Now I feel betrayed because I thought you wanted me to always say "yes" to you.

-Deonte' Earl Towner

Secretly Unhappy: please don't tell

double vision

I had a vision of us together forever in the future. We were going to have a huge house, a few dogs with a white picket fence. The grass was going to always be perfectly cut. The flowers in our garden were going to make people stop and stare for hours. Whenever a new neighbor would move in we would go over as a family and drop off a chocolate cake.

But all along you had different plans.

The plans didn't involve me.

You had plans with someone else. I was just your option for now. When you found someone better than me you took that opportunity to leave and not look back.

-Deonte' Earl Towner

Secretly Unhappy: please don't tell

you changed

Who Did It?

Where did you go?

Where can I find you?

Will the real you please stand up?

Who told you to become someone else?

Who told you to stop being you?

Who took your smile away and turned it into a frown?

How long did you pretend to be someone you weren't?

-Deonte' Earl Towner

Secretly Unhappy: please don't tell

taking responsibility

The way I ended things with you wasn't cool at all. I should've had more respect for you because you gave me so much. I wasn't thinking about your feelings during that time. For the past few days I have been thinking about you and the way you have changed my life for the better. I want to give it another try. I need to stop giving up on us whenever we get into arguments. My whole life I have walked away. My parents walked away when things got tough. Maybe I don't know how to love you.

Maybe I don't know how to be in a relationship.

Maybe I don't love myself.

Maybe all I care about is the money and drugs.

Or, maybe all I care about is myself and what others have to offer me. Either way I keep hurting people in the process, and I don't want to be that person anymore. The more I hurt others, the more I hurt myself. Sometimes I don't want to live anymore because I feel that if I die then it will stop me from hurting the ones I love. I want to change, but I have been like this for too long.

-Deonte' Earl Towner

Secretly Unhappy: please don't tell

confessions

You I thought I loved you but I only said it because I knew that's what you wanted me to say. You said it first and so I said it back. You were the first person I said it to and I learned never to say it unless you mean it. I didn't mean it and you know that. You are a smart person. When I said it back you knew for a fact that you didn't feel anything. You only pretended to feel the warmth because you didn't want to accept the harsh truth and reality that I didn't love you. I care about you, but I don't love you. Even though I don't love you like that I still got you anytime you need me. You gave me so much and the least I can do is be there for you.

-Deonte' Earl Towner

Secretly Unhappy: please don't tell

answer the phone

I know you are probably crying on your pillow and pretending that I don't exist. I saw that you blocked me on all social media platforms and I don't blame you. I would've done the same if I was in your shoes. You're going through a lot of family problems right now and I left you in your time of need. You got to understand that there is never a perfect time to let someone go. It wasn't easy for me to break the news. You have been strong your whole life, and you will be stronger without me.

-Deonte' Earl Towner

Secretly Unhappy: please don't tell

that's it

Since you aren't answering I won't reach out anymore.

You know how I feel, and I don't want to keep trying to be there for someone that obviously doesn't want me to be. I can be there for anyone else in the world and you keep denying my presence. I need to move on. I deserve happiness even though I caused you all this pain. You are making me mad because you keep ignoring my calls. I go to sleep thinking about you. I don't know how you are feeling right now because you haven't posted on social media. You always pretended that you were fine when things were hard.

I actually think I broke you this time and it's not a good feeling.

-Deonte' Earl Towner

Secretly Unhappy: please don't tell

reverse psychology

You never took responsibility for what you've done. I have hurt you, cheated on you and betrayed you many times but you don't have to leave me hanging. Love is patient. You should wait around for me to change. Change isn't easy but you should have some type of sympathy for me. Everyone in my life has left. My family walked out on me and now you.

I thought you told me that you will always be there for me.

I thought you told me that you would never switch up on me.

I thought you told me that we will always be together no matter what. I have a lot of issues but it won't always be like this. One day I will act right and you don't have to cry anymore. Maybe you aren't strong enough for me. Maybe you were the wrong one from the start. You will never get it. No one ever has. I swear I thought you were different. I hope you feel crappy.

It's cool.

I'm used to it. Everyone always walks out on me.

-Deonte' Earl Towner

Secretly Unhappy: please don't tell

chill out

Good morning my love. I know this morning is hard for you. You probably can't get out of bed because of what you found out last night when you were looking through my phone. I swear you mean everything to me. Not them! I was just having a conversation: nothing major. They were just pictures. I never asked for them.

-Deonte' Earl Towner

Secretly Unhappy: please don't tell

blinded

I am not strong enough to let you go, but I won't tolerate the abuse anymore. Everyone is telling me to walk away from you, but I don't want to. If I walk away from you then someone else will take my place. I have cried over you too long for someone else to have you.

I want to stay being your victim.

I will stay even if that means that you keep hurting me. Do you understand that I cry every time I stare at our conversations at night? I get no sleep because I am trying to figure out what I did wrong even though it was your fault.

-Deonte' Earl Towner

Secretly Unhappy: please don't tell

Changing

We need to talk.

I know that I told you that I loved you and I want to be in your life forever, but my feelings are beginning to change. It's not you... it's me. I haven't been feeling myself these past few weeks. We've been arguing a lot and I am picking fights with you just because. I think we should take a break and see what happens. I know this message will probably catch you by surprise because you're a fighter and I have always admired that about you. You will fight to make us work, but I do not have any fight left inside of me. I have become exhausted and I am slacking in every part of my life. I need to refocus, and in order for me to get my life back on track then I will have to let you go. You are very understanding and I know that you will be able to understand this message. You probably won't call me back after you hear this message. Just know that I still love you...

-Deonte' Earl Towner

Secretly Unhappy: please don't tell

one sided

Does your family still mention my name?

Do they ever ask about me? I miss all of them because they were there for me when my blood family wasn't. Do they think that I am a fool for letting you go? They probably all hate me and think that I am trash. If I see them in public would they say hi back? Or, will they turn away with disgust because of how I treated you?

I take it back, you probably lied on me. You probably didn't tell them the part you played. You probably painted a one sided picture of me. Tell them the whole truth. Tell them how I forgave you for things I wouldn't tell another soul. Let them judge you like they judge me.

-Deonte' Earl Towner

Secretly Unhappy: please don't tell

rumor has it

I talked to some of your friends today.

They told me that you still talk about me randomly at night when you're in the car coming from parties. I know you still cry all night after you've had a good time with your friends. I heard you were dancing on other people. I bet they can't do it like I do it. I bet they can't touch you like I touch you. I bet you wish you still had me. That is why you are pretending to be happier than you are. Who are you fooling? You surround yourself with a lot of people because you can't stand the thought of being alone. When you are alone that is when I appear in your head. I hope my thoughts haunt you. I hope when you find someone new you still think of me.

-Deonte' Earl Towner

Secretly Unhappy: please don't tell

the eyes never lie

You smile at me in public, but I can still see the pain in your eyes. You walk with so much confidence, but the silent tears you cry are still glistening in your eyes from the night before. Sometimes you wear sunglasses because you don't want anyone to see how you truly feel because you don't want anyone to think you are weak. You find yourself day dreaming throughout the day because you are still in disbelief that it's over. You tell yourself repeatedly to think positive thoughts to get through the day. No matter how many positive thoughts you have it won't bring us back. We were only meant for a season and you have to accept that. I moved on and I am so much happier. I am happier with myself and my new partner. I love you enough to tell you that it's time to move on and stop wallowing over my absence.

-Deonte' Earl Towner

Secretly Unhappy: please don't tell

Leave me alone

I have love for you still but I am not in love with you. Don't think you can just call or text me anytime you want. We aren't like that anymore. Whenever you are having a bad day don't reach out to me. We aren't a team anymore. You should've thought about that when you were acting single. You need to learn your lesson. I hope someone hurts you like you hurt me. It's hard because I pretend to act tough, but really I don't want you to get hurt. I want to protect you even though you didn't protect me. I want to wrap my arms around you and still call you mine. I am loyal to you even though you set me free. I just want you to feel my pain. Make me feel wanted and needed. I hate seeing you happy without me. I hate seeing you doing your own thing without me by your side. Do you care that I am dying on the inside. I am fighting an endless war on the inside over you. The burning I feel in my chest, the waves I feel in my stomach. It is becoming too much. I just want to scream in exhaustion.

-Deonte' Earl Towner

Secretly Unhappy: please don't tell

facing reality

I have random thoughts about being in your warm embrace, but then all the memories of how you ever did me takes over and gives me a bitter feeling on the inside.

-Deonte' Earl Towner

Secretly Unhappy: please don't tell

listen

Sorry for all the times I hurt you,

for all the pain I caused,

for all the tears you shed,

for all the times you put up with my abuse,

for all the times you were looking out for me and I pushed you away,

for all the times I ignored you when all you showed was concern,

for all the times you punished yourself in order to love me...

I'm sorry.

-Deonte' Earl Towner

Secretly Unhappy: please don't tell

new perspective

I didn't realize how bad I treated you until someone did the same thing to me that I did to you.

Now I can properly apologize for my behavior.

Now I see where you were coming from.

Now I understand all the tears you shed over me.

Now I see why it took you so long to move on.

-Deonte' Earl Towner

Secretly Unhappy: please don't tell

emotional support

Are you available right now? I am assuming that you are busy. I know we haven't talked in a year but I need you. This message probably caught you by surprise. I am going through some hard times in my life and I can't go through this alone. My new partner doesn't understand me because we are barely building a foundation. They don't understand my life and what I have been through like you do. I know you have moved on and in a happier place. Things didn't end well, but can we put all of our differences to the side? Please just be there for me tonight.

-Deonte' Earl Towner

Secretly Unhappy: please don't tell

finally hitting me

You are no longer mine anymore, and I am no longer yours. At work today I had to take a quick break and cry because it is finally hitting me that we aren't together anymore.

I don't get to see you after the day is gone.

I don't get to wake up to a text from you.

You won't call me when I am stuck in traffic.

I can't look forward to getting your warm hugs after I tell you about how unfair the day was towards me.

I wonder how long these emotions are going to last so I can refocus and get back to feeling free on the inside. My mind, body and spirit longs for your presence. I have to keep telling myself that you aren't coming back and that I am over you.. but in reality my whole world is feeling the effects that you are gone and not coming back.

-Deonte' Earl Towner

Secretly Unhappy: please don't tell

again

It feels good that we are talking again, but you're only reaching out to me because you are lonely and everyone has left your life. I never thought in a million years we would talk again but I know you are only using me. You will leave me again when someone else better comes along. I am tired of being used all the time. I come at the command of your voice. No matter what I will always be here for you, even if that means being hurt all the time.

-Deonte' Earl Towner

Secretly Unhappy: please don't tell

it's official

I recently deleted all of our pictures together. I deleted all of our old text messages because I kept reading them repeatedly at night. I would smile and then get sad because it wasn't the same anymore. Things will never go back to how it used to be.

We tried to talk on the phone and retell old jokes but I could tell that you were forcing a laugh.

We went out to dinner and all you could hear were the plates making noises.

We tried so hard to rekindle what we lost. But once feelings change you can't get them back sometimes. My feelings needed to get hurt again for me to realize it's officially over.

-Deonte' Earl Towner

Secretly Unhappy: please don't tell

the last phone call

When we see each other in public can we at least act cordial. You're in a relationship and I am too. I still have feelings for you, and I know you have them for me. We can't act upon them because we are too toxic for each other. When you see me around, and you smile at me...

Are you smiling because you are thinking about all of our memories we had together?

Are you smiling because you are pretending that you aren't hurt anymore and you want to convince me that you are happier?

Or, are you smiling because you have finally moved on? Even though I am in a relationship it hurts because I will never move on. They always say that there is nothing like your first love. If we could go back in time would we do it different? If you knew how things would end would you have still given me a chance? If you gave me one more night would it be passionate and will that give me the closure that I need? I guess I will never know.

-Deonte' Earl Towner

Secretly Unhappy: please don't tell

Secretly Unhappy: please don't tell

Acknowledgments:

Thank you to Jesus Christ who is the head of my life. He has been by my side every step of the way. When I was on the verge of committing suicide he stopped me before it was too late.

I thank God for my beautiful parents Joseph and Emily Towner. I have always considered them my best friend. I talk to them on the phone three to four times a day. We have an unbreakable bond.

To my siblings Nina and Jojo. Thanks to my big sister Nina for always making me laugh during times that were meant to be serious. Thanks to my big brother Jojo for always freeing me in times I felt overwhelmed by the burdens of life.

To my grandmother we call Big Momma. You remind me that no matter how old I get I am still your big ol baby. Thanks for making me feel like a kid..

To my beautiful readers in Salinas, the 831 and everyone around the world. You all remind me every day that I am not alone. There are people out there that struggle and go through it every day. Let's continue to lift each other up in prayer. We are strong, we are warriors. You all are my friends and family.

Made in the USA
Coppell, TX
10 December 2019